HAPPY NEW

by
Brendan Cowell

Published by Playdead Press 2013

© Brendan Cowell

Brendan Cowell has asserted his rights under the
Copyright, Design and Patents Act, 1988, to be
identified as the author of this work.

A CIP catalogue record for this book is available from
the British Library.

ISBN 978-0-9576077-9-8

Printed by BPUK

Playdead Press
www.playdeadpress.com

Happy New received its Australian Premiere produced by Rouge Star Productions at the Old Fitz Theatre, Woolloomooloo, Sydney in 2002 with the following cast:

Danny   Anthony Hayes
Lyle   Brendan Cowell
Pru   Blazey Best

Director   Leland Kean

Happy New received its UK premiere produced by Inside Intelligence on 31 January 2012 at The Old Red Lion Theatre, St John Street, London EC1, with the following cast:

Danny	Alfred Enoch
Lyle	Joel Samuels
Pru	Josie Taylor

Director and Producer	Robert Shaw
Designer	Claire Lyth
Lighting	Richard Williamson
Sound	Chris Pavlo
Stage Manager	Carla Batten
Fight Arranger	Kristina Søeborg
Production Assistant	Sophie Wilding

The production extended by four weeks from 28 February 2012:

Danny	Alfred Enoch
Lyle	Ed Birch
Pru	Helen Duff

Stage Manager	Bex Keable-Crouch

Inside Intelligence's production of *Happy New* opened in the West End at Trafalgar Studios on 4 June 2013:

Danny	William Troughton
Lyle	Joel Samuels
Pru	Lisa Dillon

Director	Robert Shaw
Producer	Chris Foxon
Designer	Lily Arnold
Lighting	Johanna Town
Sound	Chris Pavlo
Stage Manager	Sarah Rhodes Cannings
Fight Arranger	Kristina Søeborg
Assistant Director	Alice Kornitzer

Happy New would not have been possible without its generous sponsors: The Foyle Foundation, The Boris Karloff Charitable Trust, Mrs Margaret Guido's Charitable Trust, The Coutts Charitable Trust, Judi Dench, Kirsten Rausing, Tom Stoppard, Joanna Lumley, Richard Wilson, Jeremy Irons and Melvyn Bragg

The producers would like to extend special thanks to Nando's for supplying generous quantities of delicious BBQ chicken.

Author's note

'Happy New is my second play, written in 2001 when I was 24 years old. The play was inspired by a newspaper story I read in high school about two school boys who were locked in a chicken pen and abandoned by their mother. Who would have known this image would haunt me ten years later when I was considering a new work. I am very grateful to the actors who helped me develop this text at that time. Blazey Best, Anthony Hayes, Darren Weller, and the Director of the Tamarama Rock Surfers, Leland Kean. I am also indebted to all who were involved in that incredible era at a little pub theatre in Sydney called 'The Old Fitzroy', which will never be forgotten by all who cut their teeth there in the early 2000's. Twelve years later I cannot believe the play is debuting on the West End, and for this I thank Robert Shaw alone, who read this play 5 years ago and of all my works was intent on staging 'the chicken play'. It has been a long road to the Trafalgar but thanks to Robert and Inside Intelligence this disturbing comedy about sibling rivalry and the victims our media choose to forget, is here for London to see. Where I am from, in Cronulla, Sydney, a lot of young men don't make it out of their youth, they spend their short lives in a silent hell surrounded by inexplicable natural beauty and seemingly ideal middle class happiness. What darkness stirs inside young men has always been of great importance to my work, and I hope this piece gives light to the sweetness which lives within all the lost boys of our world."
Brendan Cowell, 2013

ACT ONE

**Two beds and a window. A large empty bowl in the center
of stage. On the wall a framed and signed photograph of
John Farnham. DANNY and LYLE sit. They have exfoliant
face masks on and are very still. They hold peeled bananas.**

Long Silence.

DANNY: Eat.

LYLE: Eating.

*Lyle rips into his banana. Danny nibbles at his. Lyle finishes
his banana. Lets it digest.*

LYLE: Oh fuck.

DANNY: Yep.

Pause.

LYLE: What are we currently experiencing?

DANNY: An all natural, anti-bacterial face mask
designed to cleanse the skin of excess oil, extract deadness,
and repel impurities. Formulated with Jamaican Triclosan
to help inhibit bacteria on the skin's surface and prevent
future skin weirdness. No more weirdness. Contains
exclusive Skin Response Complex of Balm mint,
Lemonflower, and camphor to soothe, absolve, and deeply
nurture the skin. An earthy activity, this exfoliant re-feuls
and re-births the skin, and the human, welcoming and
escorting the human into a cleaner, more prodigal happy

7

new lifestyle, where nothing... And I mean nothing, can go wrong.

Silence. The men begin to click their fingers in time, and sway from side to side in a slow, jazzy way.

DANNY: *(singing)* Happy new...

LYLE: *(singing)* Life!

DANNY: *(singing)* Happy new...

LYLE: *(singing)* Year!

DANNY: *(singing)* Happy new...

LYLE: *(singing)* Face!

DANNY and Lyle stand up.

DANNY and LYLE: HAPPY NEW MEEEEEE!!

They hold the note, finish, then sit back down. Silence.

DANNY: I preferred the clay mask. Was that last year?

LYLE: Clay mask was last year. Peach mask the year before. And something very odd the year before that. Something Tibetan, like yack urine, or Goat urine... Made me look like Brian Henderson.

DANNY: Clay mask was fantastic. Last year was fantastic. Clay mask was fantastic. This lemonflower one, it's so...

LYLE: Clay mask was fantastic, this one's so…
lemonflower… it's so…

DANNY: Drippy oily.

LYLE: Drippy oily!

DANNY: I feel like a salad, and there's this
Balsamic dirty… Dirty, dirty balsamic dressing dripping
down my face like some kind of slutty lemonflower.

LYLE: Impure.

DANNY: I'm a salad.

LYLE: We're just salad.

DANNY: You can feel it working though.

LYLE: Oh it's fantastic, clay mask was fantastic,
lemonflower's fantastic.

DANNY: You can feel it sucking out all the shit
from your head, just sucking the fuck out of you. Such a
brilliant thing to do at this time of year. Especially a year
like this. Suck the fuck out of this year.

LYLE: What a year.

DANNY: What a year.

Pause.

DANNY: What a gloriously sordid year. What a crowded year. This year had no scaffolding, just filth and change and rubbing.

LYLE: Chaos.

DANNY: Madness. Mistakes. I made so many wonderful mistakes in every aspect of my life.

LYLE: You sure did.

DANNY: And I learnt nothing. Which, in itself, is the greatest mistake.

LYLE: The harbour bridge of mistakes.

DANNY: And dark!

LYLE: Pitch black!

DANNY: Little or no light. A deep, richly sombre year clouded with gregarious women, junk mail, and constant breakages.

LYLE: Bang! Crash!

DANNY: Smash!

Pause. Danny finishes his banana, holds onto the peel.

LYLE: And then it was over.

DANNY: Lyle.

LYLE: The banana all gone.

DANNY: Hey!

LYLE: What's going to happen to us?

DANNY: We're coming down the mountain now, Lyle boy, we'll get a real flow going soon. A little more time, a little more purification, we'll be living the dream.

LYLE: The Australian dream?

Pause.

LYLE: What a year.

DANNY: What a face mask.

LYLE: Clay mask was fantastic.

DANNY: A good year begins with a good face mask.

LYLE: What will this year hold?

Lyle looks at Danny. Pause.

DANNY: Fuck.

LYLE: Fuck!

DANNY: Next year I'll lie less, tell the truth more, smoke less, drink more mineral water. Call my dentist, read more, rise earlier. Research dogs, maybe get one, work a job, dream less, smile when I leave the house, smile when I answer the phone, smile when I trip up the pavement, smile when I lose my wallet. Smile. It's almost the new year. I should see it as it is. The sun has spun its wobbly

11

frame around the earth again and it is time to have a little look inside one's self and muster a plan for what's to come! Next year I will get more sun and kill more opportunities. Next year I will let people in. Next year I'll diarise, filofax, keep appointments, keep the car clean, make more mix tapes, one's that Pru likes as well, a happy medium, oh God Pru. Next year, one word: monogamy. Monogamy. Live the Australian dream. Keep my eyes straighter. Lean a little more towards the possibility of coupledom, of true coalition. Give love some cash to spend. Put a couple of fivers in the old love account. Y'know. Next year.

Silence.

LYLE: Next year I spend more time with you. Next year I travel.

DANNY: The islands, the coast, Indonesia...

LYLE: No, just around the suburb a bit more. I tend to spend a lot of time in the flat.

DANNY: You've never left the flat.

LYLE: I glow I'm that white. I stuck my head out the window the other day and the postie crashed into the tree. I was emanating massive voltages of glare. Extremely disconcerting experience. Must travel. I've thought about fake tan but I'm no fake.

DANNY: You're the real thing.

LYLE: You're the real thing.

Clanging noise.

DANNY: It's not.

LYLE: It can't be.

DANNY: She said...

LYLE: The party...

DANNY: It's her...

LYLE: Definitely her...

DANNY: Climbing the stairs...

LYLE: So ambitious...

DANNY: You can feel the Gym membership from the way she takes the corners.

LYLE: She's a treadmill.

DANNY: She's a chainsaw.

LYLE: Legs like condominiums.

DANNY: Breasts like amplifiers.

LYLE: And a heart...

DANNY: Like an empty pouch of tobacco.

LYLE: And eyes...

DANNY: Like two competitive factory outlets.

LYLE: And hair…

DANNY: Like a waterfall.

LYLE: A princess.

DANNY: A glorified fucking angel.

LYLE: The love of your life.

DANNY: And mine.

Louder, closer clanging. Enter Pru. Pause.

PRU: I am very angry! I've been angry, am angry, and will continue to be angry. I left the party with anger, drove across town with anger, bought sashimi with anger, the whole time thinking about you, and her, and now we are three… and anger, all over me like a fierce rash. I approach the angry stairwell from the angry streets with angry amounts of wasabi beating down my head like a menstrual samurai. Angry as fuck! Angry as a victim. And here I am, so completely made of anger that I feel at any moment I will combust, flinging angry pieces of Pru all over these bulging walls. That is me. That is what you have made of me. That's what you have done. You absolute cunt!

Pru points out the window.

PRU: And of all the women in this sordid town you chose her.

Pause.

PRU: I was at the party and I craved you, was
hit by a pang of you, whilst sipping good Champagne in a
good conversation, you, the love, hit me. So I excuse my
pissy self and take the elevator down to the car park, the
trill of a million conversations warbling in my head. I find
the car, fumble with the keys, I hear a noise, turn to see
my boss and the new accounts manager fucking on his
Statesman, I throw them a look, he gestures like the walrus
he is, but that's extraneous, I enter the car, our car, to lie
down, in the quiet, and call you, call my love, my baby
love, it's New Years Eve, I wanna' talk to my baby. And
Aaaaarrgghhhh!! Fuuuuccckkkk!! A sudden, excruciating
shaft of agony ripples through my arse and up my spine,
throwing tears from my eyes and waves of pain through
my body. What could it be? Candelabra? No. Not in our
car. A 16th century sword from the battle of Main? No. An
echidna? No. Well, what is it then I hear you ask that's
jutting into my arse? I'll fucking tell you what it is.

Pru holds up a loop earring.

PRU: A cheap as shit, plastic, summer Sportsgirl
loop earring worn only by one woman.

Silence. Pru looks out the window.

PRU: And I know, from the small window of my
mercenary life I can see, that not even bad traffic can
unstick an earring. I know, by the way the earring poked
garishly out of the back seat, that it had come loose by the
force of erotic pleasure, of sexual duress, and I know, you
have been on her and in her in our car that we bought on
line for a steal at twice the price... And you don't even
drive the thing, so, in my keenest Angela Lansbury

reckoning, you've made the mess in a still car, below the window of your battery life.

Pause.

PRU: I don't know what I'm doing here. I don't know what else I have to say. But, to tell you... that you've killed me. My heart. You've killed it. I'm all black inside now, and I don't think I can see you again. I loved you with everything I had and who else? Who else ever gave a half a fuck for you too clucking mong-tards?

Pause.

PRU: I love big because it's the only way, but it's times like these I wish I didn't. I wish I kept no one in here but myself. I let you in, un-protected, no bouncers, no security guards, unbridled I let you live in my heart... and you stuff that bitch like the putrid olive she is!? How does that make me feel!? Like an empty bladder of cask wine. I've heard of this kind of pain, but now it's here I know it's dimensions, and I'm weak to it, you've killed me, and us. Now we are three. You absolute cunt!

Pause. DANNY goes to get up.

PRU: All the lemonflower antioxidant grape seed extract aloe gel camphor resin in the world won't cleanse this dirty act of betrayal and fuckededness.

Pause. Goes to leave, doesn't.

PRU: Are you young? Is that what it is? Or are you just plain fucking stupid? Do I mean that little to you? All those whispers as we fall to sleep, are they all lies? All the talk of dogs and filofax's and smiling, is that all shit? Am I meant to believe any of what you've said to me? Was it worth it!? I hope it was, I hope it was the best fuck you ever had cos' it just cost you the one and only good thing you had in your life. Me! No more me in your life, no more marriage, no more house in the country, no more piano, no more three kids, eight dogs and warm summer salads with goats cheese and semi roasted conversations deep into the night. No more squeezing. No more music and wine and kissing. You've killed us with one thrust of your meandering sword. Dead. The love of my life. Dead.

Pause. Pru leaves. Pause. Pru re-enters.

PRU: And, oh, silly me, is that it or have I stumbled upon a hobby? Is she the only one? Was that the only time? Have you been throwing your cock around all year? After I nurse you to your teary sleep do you slip out and fuck some scrubber? I don't understand you I fucking don't! I am sweet am I not? I am intelligent, focussed, warm, engaging, I have three email addresses and a deposit on an art deco studio warehouse slash living space apartment in lower Castlecrag, I have fantastic tits, great skin, a well fed sense of humour, I have structure, I work hard, I'm driven. What more do you need? Want!? You told me, oh my God it's all becoming clear as day now. Just last week you told me you loved me so much it kept you awake. You said to me, "Pru, I am so in love, I am so happy and new".

Pru pours gin into a glass.

PRU: It's enlightening to know your only capacity for romance or flattery is a direct result of guilt.

Pru skulls her gin. Tops it back up.

PRU: Right, well, you can sit here in an empty room with your empty brother and exfoliate til' your face falls off, I'm going to go back to the party and the first man I see I'm going to escort him to the amenities and throw him into a cubicle and I'm going to ride him like a cowgirl out of hell!

Pause. Pru slugs the last of her gin, and drops the glass so it smashes.

PRU: Fuck you, you fucking cunt!

Pru leaves. Clanging. Long silence.

LYLE: She's a little upset.

DANNY: Mildly.

LYLE: Whoah.

DANNY: Women.

LYLE: Whoah.

Pause.

LYLE: You fucked up.

DANNY: Shut up.

Pause.

LYLE: One could say you have egg on your face,
but you don't. You have lemonflower balm mint.

DANNY: Shut up.

Pause.

LYLE: You can't break up. That'd kill me.

DANNY: Shut the fuck up.

Pause.

LYLE: How do you feel about yourself right now?
Do you like effecting people like that? Do you like
watching them spin?

Pause. Danny exits to wash his face.

LYLE: It was just a matter of time you know.
Before she made the discovery. No one can conceal secrets
like that, they're too big, they reveal themselves. I believe
there's hope though, you know, I measured a little hope, a
little glimpse of forgiveness and positivity in a couple of
her closing remarks. Don't throw the towel in right away.
Time heals Danny, just keep moisturising, keep up the
fluids. She was brought up by the sea Danny and that's got
to move her in some way to the fulcrum of understanding
and forgiveness. She loves you Danny, and love can sort its
shit out if it wants to, if it really wants to. We've got good
excuses for dirty acts, we spent a lot of time in dirt, as dirt,
we can be forgiven for random acts of broken dirtiness. It's
intrinsic.

Pause.

19

LYLE: That poor little lamb is in a great deal of pain right now. Love really hurts doesn't it? Does it Danny? I mean I wouldn't know, I've just been mounted and ridden by a woman in a tennis dress.

Pause.

LYLE: She looked fantastic though didn't she, all that stuff about anger, that was great. Will she still come around and bring things? Is it over between her and I as well? What are the rules Danny? Who made the rules? You should talk to the rule maker Danny, you just broke some of his plates. You shouldn't have done what you did Danny, I told you that, after you did it, I said Danny you just did something you shouldn't have and you said, "Lyle, that's what we call mistakes, and I just made one". And you smiled and we put paw paw oil on our arms. We've had some special times. Clean, pure, times. What's going to happen to us now? Without her. She is the only one we know. She was the only one who could help us out there.

Pause.

LYLE: She must understand, we, we've suffered, they told us we'd do things like this, they told us we'd push people away, they told us that, we're not trustable because we had an irregular phase and hence push people away when they get too close. Why haven't we pushed each other away? Why not? We're ball and socket that's why. We need one for the other. We had an irregular phase. Let's blame it on that. Blame everything on that!

Silence. Danny enters, clean faced.

LYLE: Wow, you're face is really glowing. You look tops!

DANNY: I look replenished yeah?

LYLE: You look like a whole new man.

DANNY: I feel like a whole new man. That's what a kick in the mouth and a little bit of lemonflower can do.

LYLE: I'm going to wash mine off too. I wanna' feel how you look.

Lyle leaves to wash his face.

DANNY: Look at all this glass. Broken Pru on the floor.

Pause. Danny cleans up the glass.

DANNY: So messy. A little bit of glass and the whole place looks so messy.

LYLE: *(off)* I feel a little sad.

DANNY: Yeah...

LYLE: *(off)* What did you do it for Danny? I mean really, why did you do it? You didn't need to.

Pause.

LYLE: *(off)* Danny, why'd you do it?

DANNY: That's what it's like to be in love Lyle. It's like waiting for a vase to smash. The moment where it leaves the hand, just before it hits the floor.

Pause. Danny puts on one cricket glove. Sounds of facial scrubbing and sink running.

DANNY: I have a dick Lyle, and my dick has no feelings, my dick talks its way up my body and I hear from it Lyle, I hear from it.

Pause. Danny puts on another cricket glove.

DANNY: In the place we couldn't hear anyone. It was dark and we were all broken and broken people can't hear from each other.

Pause.

DANNY: Fuck I fucked up! She'll be back. She has things here. Me, and things.

Pause. Enter Lyle, fresh faced.

DANNY: Have you anything more to say on the matter my little moral-warrior-brother-cunt?

Pause. Danny picks up a bat.

DANNY: Let's make some punch.

LYLE: Nice idea. How do I look?

DANNY: Effervescent. Punch?

LYLE: ONE LAST PUNCH!

In this sequence, Danny swings the bat naming the ingredients as Lyle adds them to the large punch bowl.

DANNY: Big bowl. Big Happy New Years Punch bowl. Big new punch.

LYLE: Let's make punch work!

DANNY: Let's work with punch.

LYLE: Punch my shit up now you filthy punch maker!

DANNY: This year's ingredients.

LYLE: Punch me silly.

DANNY: One litre of Gin.

LYLE: Punch! Ouch! Oh, you hurt me!

DANNY: A packet of kippers.

LYLE: Kippers, fishy punch.

DANNY: One jar of marmite.

LYLE: Marmite. Give it some tang.

DANNY: A small pot plant. A gift from Pru. Pruuuuuu...

LYLE: Get the broken tree in the punch.

23

DANNY: One West Coast cooler.

LYLE: Heading for the West Coast with the punch.

DANNY: Some sun screen. Factor 35.

LYLE: Protect the punch, care for the punch.

DANNY: A tin of paint.

LYLE: Spanish magenta punch.

DANNY: Your leather jacket.

LYLE: But no. Not my leather jacket.

DANNY: Off your back. Give the punch some style.

LYLE: But it's my jacket, my leather jacket.

DANNY: Nothing is owned. Release yourself, own nothing. Give to the punch.

LYLE: Oh, punch, you eclectic weird luna punch, have the jacket off my back.

Lyle puts his jacket in the punch.

DANNY: Good man! Giving makes you richer... Some withdrawal receipts.

LYLE: Invest in the punch. Think about tomorrow. Put some punch away for the future.

DANNY: A pair of Pru's top shelf knickers.

LYLE: High-class portfolio panties. Televised punch.

DANNY: Some self-esteem.

LYLE: Self-esteem.

They stare into the punch, beaming esteem energy into it.

DANNY: A litre of anti freeze.

LYLE: Again, we're looking out for the punch, caring for the punch.

DANNY: And all the hair I shaved from my face in the last twelve months.

LYLE: Shed the onion. New life. New punch.

DANNY: Two banana peels.

LYLE: Skin of the yellow goddess. *(together)* Bunana Bunana.

DANNY: And we stir.

Danny stirs the punch with a cricket bat.

DANNY: Dear punch.

LYLE: Hear our prayer.

DANNY: Are you interested in buying into me.

LYLE: I'm bleeding like a flathead plucked from the sea.

DANNY: Proffer something

LYLE: Or just repeat after me.

DANNY: I'm in love.

LYLE: With a broken candle.

DANNY: I'm in love.

LYLE: And our Para Olympic sex, it screams of clarity.

DANNY: And like butter we melt into the easy.

LYLE: Fucking traffic of the opal.

DANNY: Ironic Sydney (Do you want this to be London?)

LYLE: Baby sweet baby.

DANNY: Your job has turned you into a spreadsheet.

LYLE: And now you keep a tab on me.

DANNY: Close me down like winter.

LYLE: Close me down like winter.

DANNY: I got life at nine o'clock.

LYLE:	But I'll probably sleep in.
DANNY:	I got life at ten o'clock.
LYLE:	But I'll probably sleep in.
DANNY:	I remember how you'd come around.
LYLE:	Turn me on like a hair straightener.
DANNY:	Make me water drenched in woman.
LYLE:	Water drenched in woman.
DANNY:	You ask me why I'm hurting.
LYLE:	Its cos' you loved me in third person.
DANNY:	Baby sweet baby.
LYLE:	I'm so sorry.
DANNY:	I had supper between the legs of an idiot.
LYLE:	Baby sweet baby.
DANNY:	I'm the cigarette you can't throw.
LYLE:	I'm the cigarette that tastes of sugar.
DANNY:	I want a world of smoke and colour.
LYLE:	Round panels of light.
DANNY:	No more black black dreams.

LYLE: Of clucking in the dark.

DANNY: Of chicken pen asylum.

LYLE: Of chicken pen asylum.

LYLE: She'll be back…

DANNY: She'll be back…

Silence. Danny keeps stirring, hypnotically. Lyle is transfixed by the constant slow movement.

DANNY: Drop!

LYLE: Dropping.

LYLE drops to the floor in a heap and remains unmoved and unconscious.

Pause.

DANNY: When I'm inside a woman, I feel like I'm not a chicken. I at the very least feel like a rooster.

LYLE: Cockadoodledoo!

DANNY: You're a silly little fucker soup.

Pause.

DANNY: You follow my words like a janitor. Sweeping them up, putting them away.

Pause.

DANNY: We're getting jobs this year.

LYLE: No!

DANNY: Stand!

LYLE: Standing!

Lyle stands.

LYLE: To the office. On the train.

DANNY: A corporate man with a corporate title.

LYLE: Executive Corporate Officer Department
of Dreams and Laziness.

DANNY: Where's your office?

LYLE: By the photocopier I'll be, looking over
the city.

DANNY: And a suit?

LYLE: Every day a suit. Grey suit, brown suit,
blue suit, grey suit, black suit, grey suit.

DANNY: With a tie...

LYLE: That points to my penis.

DANNY: Power tie!

LYLE: I'll have an inbox and a parking spot.
Friends and associates. "Morning Lyle", they'll say.

Sixteen lines on my phone and a secretary. "Morning Mr. Lyle", she'll say. A mobile and a night life. A foccacia and a merger. Golf on Wednesday. Squash on Thursday. Weekends at the lodge. I'll wear my heart on my desk. I'll sleep in my briefcase. My delegates my intimates. My assistants my children. My secretary my pet. My car my peacock feathers. My eyes like ambitious javelin, spearing through companies as I saunter round the boardroom like the hawk with too much going on up here. I'll buy Queensland (Wales?), marry a model, fly a jet with my face on the side, I'll buy a gun, find our mother, ask her why she...

DANNY: You won't need me anymore. Not next year. You've got so much going on.

Pause.

LYLE: You think that can happen Danny? You really do?

DANNY: Think!? I know.

Pause.

LYLE: I was thinking about taking it easy again, for another year. Just following you around. Keeping a journal. Walking. Some Chi.

DANNY: You can't walk around Lyle!They cut us off Lyle! We've got to work. We've got to get out. You heard her. They say we're okay now. They say we can do it.

LYLE: They say a lot of shit.

DANNY: They do.

Pause.

DANNY: I believe in you Lyle. Like I believe in this
punch.

LYLE: Will you have a job? Next year?

DANNY: Of course.

LYLE: What will your line be?

DANNY: Consultant, brochures, finish the law
degree. A blend of, maybe. Use the acumen acquired from
these flip flop years of junk mail and watching. Something
useful, to be of use would be a pleasant surprise.

A car screeches to halt. Lyle rushes to look out the window.

LYLE: It's her. It's Pru. She's parked the car on
the gutter. She's getting out. She's unbuttoning her blouse
and shuffling with her dress.

DANNY: She's concocting.

LYLE: She's messing up her hair.

DANNY: She's gonna' have a story. About a man.
She's just trying to look the part.

LYLE: It looks awful out there.

DANNY: Inclement, is it?

LYLE: How are you supposed to know whether these people are men or women. They've got the heads of men and the hips of women… The man who whistles is out. And the lady with the snakes. And the guy with the turn tables. And the woman who keeps a tight ship, and the fella' with all the headphone sounds. And the young body with the old eyes. And Mr. Beautiful with the war stories. The shoplifter with the birth mark. Young Phillip and the policeman are holding hands, how modern. Bouncers with their arms on the pedestrians. Music, smashing, arms in the air, chewing their faces off. But no sportsgirl on the corner, she must be getting some loadings, it is New Years Eve.

DANNY: It's just drugs. Drugs are in. Not opera. Drugs. What's Pru doing now?

LYLE: She's ravaged herself, she looks like she's been fucked by a football team.

DANNY: That's the idea. She'll have a show, she's just in wardrobe.

Pause. Lyle turns around.

LYLE: She's entered the building.

DANNY: She'll come round, she loves punch.

LYLE: Can I just say something, before the TV cyclone blows in?

DANNY: Do.

LYLE: If everything goes black, and everything becomes nothing, if it's nothing, and there's no Happy

32

New... then I want you to know... I want you to know... That whatever you do... If whatever you want to do is what you want to do, then I'll have no hesitation in doing it with you. Even if it means...

DANNY: Of course it won't.

Louder clanging. Enter Pru.

PRU: Well stick a feather up my arse and call me a rooster how the hell are you two?

Pause.

PRU: Lovely night out. Lovely night for riding men.

Pause.

DANNY: Punch?

PRU: Maybe later. But, I'm not staying long. Just came to tell you what I've been doing, fetch a couple of things and head off into another life, away from you two viral creatures.

Pause.

DANNY: Doesn't Lyle look effervescent?

PRU: Fuck you donkey dick. Don't small talk me. You can't work your way back to this Africa baby, you lost your passport. Mama Pru-Pru's got a brand new bag.

DANNY: You've had a hard one I see? Got a leg over? In the amenity's was it?

PRU: Africa has its secrets.

DANNY: Who's Africa?

LYLE: She is. And you don't have a passport. Lost your passport.

DANNY: My passports in the linen closet. I know exactly where it is.

LYLE: She's being drunk and figurative.

DANNY: She is a drunk. She's a power suit alcoholic. She thinks she has it under control by the way she turns up to work, but I know her face, and I can see the wallpaper peeling off the walls.

LYLE: She is pastier in the daylight.

PRU: She! Is in the room. She is crying at the bar as a man slides through the traffic.

Pause.

PRU: Hey baby what's your name? – Who's asking? – I am – Well if you're asking maybe I'll tell you, my names Henry – Henry, that's a soft name for such a rugged man – Who says I'm rugged? – It's just a vibe. What department are you in? – Reality broadcasting – Oh – I call the shots in terms of what people see, I'm one of the big guys – Oh, you're wife must be very proud – My wife? Oh, I get it, that's funny – I wasn't trying to be funny –

34

Yeah, right – Have you seen the view from the women's toilets? – No, ma'am, have you seen the view from my penthouse suite upstairs? – No, but I'm intrigued – To the elevator with a hand on my ribs. Through the building we climb, in a glass elevator filled with tears and money, to the penthouse where you need passwords and sliding metal to enter, but not to enter me. My eyes close, as a hand finds my leg, and follows it's short street to my warm place, buckling my legs and flooring me, he hovers, removing my clothes with flicks of his fingers, and naked, inside carpet, I search for you, on my stomach, through the jungle of expensive shagpile, crawling like a frightened soldier, where are you Danny, and the love we made, and in the jungle, in the penthouse, there's a man on my back, and he knows me like a stranger, as he fills me full of Henry, and the world he needs to own. And thunder wakes me from my dream. The thunder of a shower, roaring like a storm in the en suite. I'm naked, tangled in remarkable sheets, and he, the storm in the shower, had me like a man. I'm driving car, our car, our earring car of infidelity, to your house, where there's never two or more things to do. And I'm driving past the bars, moving through the lights, and past the fast food drive throughs, to the chicken shop. On top of which a massive neon chicken flashes like a concert, and I'm crying, cos' I love chicken. I get out of the car, and I'm trying to climb the building to get to the massive flashing chicken. "I want to hold the chicken, I want to feel the chicken", they pull me down and I'm pathetic, waling like a child with an ice cream down it's leg. "I love chicken!" "I love chicken!" and the pavement fills with tears, and carries me to car and wooshes me back in a whirlpool. She's back An award winning woman. My names Pru. Pru. Danny, you hear that, my names Pru. Pru. Pru. My name's Pru.

Silence.

PRU: Now if I can just fetch my knickers and my fern I'll be out of here.

Pause.

LYLE: I'm in for a ginseng bath. Deep cleanse.

Lyle walks to the door.

DANNY: Who's a silly fucker?

LYLE: I am.

DANNY: Who's a silly fucker soup?

LYLE: I am.

Lyle leaves. Pause. Lyle re-enters.

LYLE: The man inside the book I read said fight for it. You know, what you want, he said fight for it.

Lyle leaves again. Pause. Sound of a bath running.

PRU: Just fetch my knickers and my fern and I'll leave you to your party.

Pause.

DANNY: Lyle needs you. You're his wall.

PRU: You know what hurts the most? You know what does. Geography. Strangely enough it's geography. You went outside for her. You left these walls for her. And all the launches and fundraisers and dinners and awards nights and parties and eloquent functions I invited you to. To get you out there and turns this sip around. And you give me bags and bags of no's. But my Sportsgirl sibling, wrapped in a stitch and ready to service, is the one thing that moves your legs down those steps. The one thing. That hurts.

Pru takes a cup and goes to pour in some punch. Pause. She pulls out her knickers.

PRU: These knickers are cutting edge fucking Prada low briefs and now they are an ingredient. Do you hold on to anything?

DANNY: Not very well, it seems. You know me Pru.

PRU: No, I don't think I do.

DANNY: This year we have throw it out. All of it. Clean the year out, make room for this new one.

PRU: Happy new...

DANNY: Happy New.

Pause.

PRU: Don't fight too hard for me Danny.

Pause. Pru tastes the punch.

PRU: Tastes like me. Tastes like your face, and Australia. Tastes like you, me, and Australia.

DANNY: Good consistency?

PRU: Moderate. Could do with more stirring.
The leather hasn't completely infused.

DANNY: Yes, leather's difficult.

Pause.

DANNY: So I guess we're even now.

PRU: How?

DANNY: In our dalliances.

PRU: Mine was a response. Yours was betrayal.

DANNY: You really know yourself don't you?

Pru lights a cigarette and sits down.

DANNY: Can I've a cigarette?

PRU: Smoke your own.

DANNY: I don't have any.

PRU: They sell them outside.

Pause.

DANNY: You want me to go out there again.
After...

PRU: Get out of here.

DANNY: Get out of where?

PRU: Out of this.

DANNY: Out of you or out of here or out of this?

PRU: Away!

DANNY: I'm leaving the house Pru, and you know
what you are? You're a witness! This is Danny, leaving the
house – for no other reason than to grab some air.

PRU: Fuck off then.

DANNY: No other reason!

PRU: Cunt go!

He does. Pru smokes.

PRU: Men are shithouse.

Pause.

PRU: Men are shithouse.

*Pause. Pru stands up and walks to the John Farnham
portrait on the wall, she talks to it.*

PRU: I bought those knickers the day of our first
date, and now they linger in the back of my throat. Is that
ironic or ludicrous? I wanted to have nice knickers, just in
case we ended up in a sizzle. But we didn't. He didn't lay a
hand on me for three months. I thought he was A-sexual. I
thought a lot of different things. When I first met him he

used to walk like a chicken. When he first came out they moved exactly like chickens for four years. It was like they were sleepwalking and if you were to wake them, they'd flip out. So they put them in a place where they slowly wittled the chickens away. Sometimes I miss his cluck, his bobbing head, his funny walk. I think that's what attracted me to him, his awkward chook-like behaviour. Now he's so upright and indifferent. There's really nothing to him. He's neither awkward nor orthodox. He's just Danny. When we first became intimate he commented on the knickers. He said they were glorious. They stayed on his floor for the rest of the year. Which in a way is a beautiful compliment. Because Danny hates mess. Hates it. To the point of neurosis.

Pause. Lyle enters, rubbing moisturiser into his skin frantically.

LYLE: Come on come on you mad fucking cream get into my pores, climb in, cleanse me, come on! Come Ooonnnnn!!! Ohhh, that feels good. Oh the shaking stops. Oh, shaking stops.

Pause. Lyle sits down.

PRU: Better?

LYLE: Ginsengs too intense. Too intense. I knew that already, but for some reason I needed to find it out again. Far too intense.

PRU: Right.

Pru goes to stand up.

LYLE: Pru, you can't leave. You simply can't.
We'd fall apart if you left. You hold us up.

PRU: That's very sweet Lyle, but...

LYLE: No but's, you have a purpose here, a
function, you're needed in this room.

PRY: And that's supposed to be everything a
woman wants.

LYLE: You won't even have to work. You can lay
around the house, drinking the finest punch and buffing
your nails. I'm going to be Corporate Motherfucker and
Danny's going into the um... he'll be of use.... you can't
leave. The future's about to change it's colour. From black
to grey to bright fucken' orange, and we want you to be a
part of it.

PRU: You're a sweet kid Lyle.

LYLE: I'm not a kid Pru.

PRU: Lyle.

LYLE: Don't call me a kid, Pru.

PRU: It just slipped out.

LYLE: I'm a big guy, I'm no child.

PRU: I know that, hell, it's just an expression,
"kid", its an expression.

LYLE: Well just don't use it on me.

PRU: Never ever again.

LYLE: So you'll stay?

PRU: I didn't say I'd stay, I just said...

LYLE: Stttaaayyyyy!!

Pause.

PRU: You know there's girls out there that'd like you Lyle. I know some. I could introduce you.

LYLE: Don't parlay Pru, don't segue.

PRU: Nice girls with nice hair and nice voices.

Pause.

PRU: Would you like that Lyle? A nice... (amorous noise)... with a nice girl?

Pause.

PRU: You could talk to them, you could even touch them.

LYLE: I don't want to touch them. I want you to stay!

Pru repeats her amorous noise.

LYLE: No girls. No more tennis.

PRU: These girls have nothing to do with tennis.

LYLE: Moisturiser.

Lyle rubs more moisturiser in.

LYLE: Ahhhh...

PRU: These girls won't do anything like that.

Pause.

LYLE: You leave, I'll put my head in the oven and turn the fan force on.

PRU: You don't need me here Lyle, you just think you do.

LYLE: You'll fucking stay you will!

Pause.

PRU: You're falling in again. Lyle.

LYLE: Up and down.

PRU: Let me tell you something.

LYLE: Something.

PRU: You and Danny...

LYLE: Danny boy.

PRU: I love the both of you so much.

LYLE: But him, it was always him.

43

PRU: He seemed stronger at the time. More defined.

LYLE: He just said less in the interview.

PRU: He formed a strong relationship with the camera, and the viewers responded to that.

LYLE: They thought I was gimpy.

PRU: That was one letter.

LYLE: You made me look gimpy. Like a gimp.

PRU: I did my best to tell the true story.

LYLE: But you said it to me, to both of us, there are no true stories on television. There's only embellishment and lies.

PRU: I showed them the real you. They wanted to exploit you, make you look like aliens.

LYLE: We are aliens!

PRU: The point I was getting to was this, it was Danny's strength, what he'd learnt from the whole thing, how far he'd come, I'd never met a man whose main force was learning.

LYLE: So you fuck him, fuck the talent, fuck the subject.

PRU: But you, I looked at you and I knew what you had, I saw it.

LYLE: You saw a gimp in a shoe box is what you saw.

PRU: I saw a man with a future, with charisma, and a keen lust for life.

LYLE: But Danny…

PRU: Okay Danny, but you, I knew it was you who had the future, the big dreams.

LYLE: I have got a couple of dreams up my sleeve. Corporate dreams.

PRU: Embrace them Lyle.

LYLE: Power. Attention. Respect. Options. Opinions.

PRU: They can all be realities.

LYLE: I don't know.

PRU: Look at me Lyle.

LYLE: Looking.

PRU: Highly   successful   woman.   Highly decorated figure.

LYLE: With some seriously undecorated friends.

PRU: I got here through sheer perseverance and drive. Nothing else.

LYLE: You have more. You glow.

PRU: Nothing else, but sheer...

LYLE: I don't feel very employable.

PRU: You have what it takes Lyle. The Australian dream is yours you just have to hold out your hands.

LYLE: Don't fill my head with the colours, Pru.

PRU: I just hate to see true talent go to waste. If I had what you have I'd be... I'd be... Somewhere else.

LYLE: There is nowhere else. No matter where I go. Inside the pen. Outside the pen. It's all the same.

PRU: It's absolutely invigorating out there.

Pause.

LYLE: Do you have your own office?

PRU: Looks over the city.

LYLE: Photocopier?

PRU: Fax, laptop, and benefits.

LYLE: Assistants?

PRU: Two assistants and a runner.

LYLE: Are the people who work nice?

46

PRU: They're a breed, not a nice breed, as time goes by they get nicer.

LYLE: The blokes in the office. Are they nice? They don't have awful laughs and foul colognes do they?

PRU: Some of them, yes.

LYLE: I couldn't endure that.

PRU: Some of them are very generous, very talented, and sometimes very encouraging.

LYLE: And you reckon I'd fit in?

PRU: They'd welcome you in as a prodigal son.

LYLE: And the girls? Are the girls nice who work?

PRU: They're lovely. They get together, talk about all kinds of things.

LYLE: Like what?

PRU: Like work and play and the future and shoes.
shoes.

LYLE: I can talk that. I could do that.

PRU: They'd eat you up.

LYLE: Lyle. 24, seeks girl with nice hair and open mind. Loves paranoia, moisturiser, and not leaving the house. Less than no sense of humour with deep psychological problems.

PRU: You'd change in the workplace, you'd fire!

LYLE: I'd be charming too, say hi to everyone as I exit the elevator, bit of rapport with the girls from accounts, wassup' to the dude from the mail room, hi-five with the marketing guy, you know, I'll be the guy everyone talks to at the Christmas Party.

PRU: Dance with you, talk to you, and maybe even...

LYLE: Oh yeah, they'll like me, cos' I feel I come from left field a little, I'm eclectic, I'm a dark horse, but a dark horse who you could introduce to your mum. Like a light brown dark horse. Nutty.

Pru walks over to him. Strokes him.

PRU: The new world is going to love you. The future's going to love you.

LYLE: Would you love me Pru? If you met me out there? Didn't know about my chicken? Would you love me?

Pru and Lyle stare at each other. They're lips almost meeting, but for -

LYLE: Can we practice a work situation? Mock one up?

PRU: Sure, yes, excellent. Shall we take it from the alarm going off in the morning, or shall we just cut straight to the office?

LYLE: Let's go straight to the office.

PRU: That's why you're going to make it, you're immediate, you're ambitious, you're...

LYLE: Let's just do this Pru, less talk, more doing.

PRU: But sir, the other party is trembling, the merger is looking shaky and managements starting to doubt our involvement.

LYLE: We have to isolate our intentions, conglomerate, get on the front foot, no more ifs and buts, 110% effort from the whole team, I can't do this on my own.

PRU: Shall I send out a group email?

LYLE: No! Fax! Fax everyone! Tell them...

PRU: Tell them?

LYLE: We're in a precarious position, we've worked so hard on this deal and we've been given a right bum steer from the delegates, but we mustn't crumble, we have to do this for the industry, and for the Australian dream.

PRU: Shall we double the offer and cut all extras?

LYLE: Precisely. But the opposite. I have a think tank with my post-integral chemist at noon, we're dining, we'll adjourn til' then, for now I ask you to keep your hands by your sides, mum's the word, and if management want to make an omelette, tell them it'll be me breaking all the eggs.

PRU: Right away Lyle, sir...

LYLE: There are three ways to tackle every situation my girl. Firstly you look it in the eye, see it for what it is, smell it, own it, research it, then you think about who you are as a person, and as an Australian, and you apply that with style and force, and thirdly...

Lyle takes Pru's hands.

LYLE: You inject every litre of everything bad that's ever happened to you, into one act of pride and power, and you stare the wolf in the eye, and overcome it. Leap, and the net will appear.

They kiss, and kiss, and kiss. Slow release. Lyle remains unmoved. Pru sits down.

LYLE: That was... I mean... that was... I've only... That was...

PRU: Nice?

LYLE: That was...

PRU: Nice?

LYLE: Years I've... Watched... that was... I mean... I've watched you... and Danny... in... Just there... kissing and... I've seen it all... Watched it... never

looked like... never looked so... Tenderness... Lost... so
lost... that was...

PRU: It was very special.

Pause. Pru goes to get up, without looking, Lyle knows.

LYLE: Don't move.

PRU: I was just going to...

LYLE: Don't fucking move.

PRU: Lyle, I'm just going to fix myself...

LYLE: No! See! No! No! That's what you do, you
love me with your lips and then you change and leave and
abrupt... things are different now. Things are very
different now. I'm not sure you should have done that. I'm
not sure you know what you've just done.

PRU: I think you may be over-reacting.

LYLE: Shut up and stay still! You will not move
and you will not speak. I'm the pecker in this room. Cluck.

PRU: Lyle, it...

LYLE: I want another one! And another one! I
want them all! Cluck.

PRU: I will come to you with another one.

LYLE: I will come to you with one of mine, cluck.

51

Pause. Lyle saunters in a spin, demurely approaches Pru in her chair, she puckers up. He glides over, clucking a little more with each step, she rises to meet his bobbing head as he grabs the bat and slams her over the head. She falls back into sitting position. Lyle starts slamming it into the ground very hard, and very consistent.

LYLE: Cluck! Cluuuuckkk!!! Cluuuuckk!!!

Lyle starts walking around with the bat, walking very chicken-like, clucking loudly.

LYLE: Clucckk!! Got my head!! Cluuucckkk!! In the wrong place!! Again!! Cluckkk!! My head's cluck!! Gone bung!! Again!! Cluck cluck!! Buck buck buckeeeehrrtt!!

Black

ACT TWO

Pru is where we left her, sitting on the floor. Enter Danny, still has his cricket gloves on.

DANNY: I went out there, oh yeah I did it, I hit the street's, and I didn't even need my gloves, and yeah, I smoked a few. Yeah, I lunged back a couple of death sticks, and I arrived at a couple of solutions. Shit, I might have another. It's New Years Eve.

Danny lights up a cigarette, it's a struggle with the gloves.

DANNY: Ya' want one?

She doesn't move.

DANNY: Fine, be coy. Fucken' crazy streets out there. Lit up and pulsating they are. Same as last year, but a little weightier. Throbbing with young people vomiting freedom into each other's mouths. It felt good out there tonight Pru. I think I'm gaining strength. I think I'm gaining self, all my planets are starting to really get along. I'm at the Picallo café, I ordered a glass of port, and I thought about you, and I thought… Fuck it's been a long road to this place. And I looked outside and it started to rain a little, and there was a guitar connected to a lady crooning velvet in the corner, and the port slid down and… Fuck it's been a long road to this place. Pru, Lyle and I… I'm sure you know… On the way back from the café I saw a woman, an old woman wandering round the pavement looking for the glasses that were hanging from one of her ears. I said to her, "Lady, if you're looking for your glasses, they're on your ear", and she looked up and she said, "I know, I know they're there, I'm just not ready to find them yet". And, I look at you, and… I mean Fuck Pru, my mother and my father had suffered war, depression, poverty, parenthood, jobs, fucken' full on things by my age. Adult things. Rivers and rivers of responsibility and I just float, selfishly, like some indulgent urban vodka, just passive, aloof, and completely obsessed with every little nuance of my meaningless and impotent life. And I float. And I float. Spend it all on me. Things to clean me, drunk me, decorate me. And I float. Over the streets and back again. To the pen. I really don't know what I'm doing here. I think about leaving but then I'd get there and see God and just say, mate, why would you want me? You don't want me in heaven, you've got heaven in a dynamic equilibrium, you've got young people, old people, brutal people, chosen people, all the demographics. I'll wreck the ambience of heaven in a matter of minutes with my modern day fucken' oblivion. I'll make everyone implode as they look to me… and see nothing. Sometimes I wish something would happen. But it never does. I understand why my mother put me in a chicken pen. She knew something needed to happen and she made it happen. That's innovation. She gave me an anecdote. And I thank her, from the more obscure section of my heart I thank her. Are you hearing all this Pru? You should be cos' it's rare I actually get a hold of so many clear thoughts at one time. Pru? Have you any response? Anything to proffer? Or are you just going to leave me here to dangle from the edge of it all like loose cotton?

Pause. Pru gets up, rips her top off and they embrace, passionately and deeply. Black.

Lights up on Pru and Danny on the floor. Their clothes are dishevelled and flung. They lay on opposite sides of the stage, panting, semi-clad. They pant in unison. Danny has one glove on.

PRU: Happy.

DANNY: Happy.

PRU: So happy.

Pause.

DANNY: This is why there are a lot of Virgo's in the world. People fuck on New Years Eve.

Pause.

PRU: Is that what we just did? Did we just fuck?

DANNY: We just fucked.

PRU: So eloquently put.

DANNY: You know what I mean.

PRU: No, I don't. I really don't.

Pause.

PRU: So Danny, you are hours from being cut off by the government, and sent out on to the streets as 'normal' members of society. How does it feel? After ten years...

Pause.

DANNY: I don't know Pru, I don't fucking know. I mean look at all these lego men and lego women. Where do I fit in that? I just float right through it. I wish they'd stop yelling, it really is not a time to be gay.

Pause. Danny yells out the window.

DANNY: There's nothing to celebrate! Stop flailing! There's nothing to celebrate!

Pause.

DANNY: There's nothing worth writing on a single t-shirt.

PRU: What about me Danny? Am I worth writing on a t-shirt?

Pause.

PRU: What would Lyle, Danny? And what about...

DANNY: Sometimes I think we can have it all, Australian Dream. Fence, house, salads, kids with quirky names, a couch with a foot rest, self respect, the whole package, I think yeah, I can see myself in the yard, with secateurs, clipping the ivy, hosing the marriage. Australian dream.

PRU: You and Lyle both?

DANNY: I haven't seen anything Pru. So, I can't see a dream. I dream of eating from my mother's face, of eating chicken cacciatore from my mother's cheek, with a blunt spoon. That's what I dream. That's all. As for the Australian Dream all I know is what Lyle tells me from reading the mail that slides under our door. We know nothing more!

PRU: Let him go Danny. Let him go.

DANNY: What?

PRU: The cage is the both of you. Alone, without him, there is no cage. Cage-free...

Pause.

A bbq chicken flies through the window. Danny goes to the window.

DANNY: Fuck off ya' cunts! Leave us alone!

PRU: Make up your mind. Quickly. Or the Australian Dream is going to take the bus just like your mother did.

Loud fast clanging. Enter Lyle, his clothes torn and bloody, soaking wet, incredibly disheveled, he holds only the handle of the bat, the rest broken off. Silence.

LYLE: Well, I'm not going out there again.

Pause.

LYLE: People don't really accept chickens. Which is wrong, cos' we invented the pecking order.

Pause.

LYLE: Chickens are members of a rigid and fixed social structure. We are either dominant or submissive. We either peck! Or we get pecked! You put an amount of birds together there will be a period of intense fighting. Pretty soon after that it will be pretty clear which bird is dominant or submissive. A bird is the shit if it pecks and the pecked bird does not peck back. At the bottom of the pecking order will be a muchly pecked bird which will be in consistently bad shape. A low bird. Watch this bird closely. Out there, exposed to light, noise, and other environmental variables, a low bird is likely to panic. Trampling, smothering, screaming, and suddenly turning against the flock. This will cause the human, who, on a night like this has been exposed to alcohol, fire works, and other confident steroids, to beat the low bird into a breakfast with many friends and hard metal implements. This is a savage act of dereliction. No one cares about chickens. Only when they're fried in a bucket by the colonel.

Pause. He looks around.

LYLE: AVOID MIXING FLOCKS and MOVING BIRDS!

Pause. He looks into the punch.

LYLE: You haven't really made a dint in the punch. I thought New Years Eve was a time to fuck yourself up. There's clothes strewn across the floor. Was there a gale? Ooh, the Soups left for a while, so let's get one on.

Pause.

LYLE: The young Soup is trying to habituate and learn but the streets don't' want him.

Pause. He picks up the bbq chicken and unwraps it, holds it up.

LYLE: Sleep, little child, sleep. They'll be here with the flash lights soon.

Pause.

LYLE: Why won't either of you say anything?!

Pause. To the bbq chicken –

LYLE: Why have we done this to you?

Pause. He pulls of a wing.

DANNY: Lyle don't!

Lyle moves it to his mouth.

PRU: Lyle simmer down, we are here for you.

DANNY: Don't do it mate.

Pause. Lyle bites from the wing.

DANNY: Fuuuck!

LYLE: Don't look at me I'm eating.

DANNY: Oh my God.

Pause.

DANNY: Lyle.

Lyle eats.

DANNY: Lyle.

Lyle eats.

DANNY: Lyle.

LYLE: I'm eating chicken for fucks sake.

DANNY: Lyle!

LYLE: You took me in there. You made me kill the first two chickens and now I'm killing the last. This is a normal sibling moment isn't it Pru?

Pause. He spits out bones.

LYLE: She always checks the cage at sunset you said. She always feeds at dawn. She always waters at midday you said. But she never ever came. The law requires that each bird have enough space to allow normal postural movement no matter what the production goals. They must have enough space to lie down, get up, stand without crouching, and freely flap their wings. Most birds are docile but do peck when left in a cage with their big brother.

DANNY: Sit down and have some punch Lyle.

LYLE: Let me do this!!

DANNY: Lyle.

Lyle cracks bones and spits them out.

DANNY: If you're eating chicken then...

PRU: Good...

Lyle throws the chicken. Danny catches it. He starts to eat it as well.

LYLE: Am I strange Pru? Tell me. Am I strange, peculiar, bizarre, freaky, a little odd Pru? Should I go see some more people about some more rhythms in my behaviour Pru? A couple more red's and white's Pru? Congentin? Largactil? Lithium? Prozac? Luvox? Zyban? Do I scare you Pru? I went from one chicken pen to another Pru. Should I jump out the window Pru?

PRU: Definitely not.

DANNY: This is fucking good chicken.

Danny eats.

DANNY: Spicy seasoning...

LYLE: Pru?

DANNY: Who's a silly fucker?! Stuffing! Wings! Breasts! Drumsticks! Marrow! Suck, the marrow! Suck

suck the marrow! Suck, the marrow! Suck suck, the marrow! There's a duty! There's a fucking duty! Suck, the marrow! Suck suck the marrow!

Pru takes lipstick from her case, draws a line on the middle of the floor, grabs Danny by the rough of his neck and forces his head towards the line so he is bent over, staring at it. He is hypnotised. Still. Silent. Pru returns to her chair, smoking, drinking, smiling out at the city. Lyle is by the punch bowl.

LYLE: Hi Pru.

PRU: Hi Lyle.

He stares at her.

LYLE: Hi Pru. Pru the kisser.

PRU: Hi Lyle.

LYLE: Lyle the kisser.

Pause. Lyle mimes a kiss at Pru.

LYLE: Hi Pru.

PRU: Hello.

LYLE: Come here, Pru.

PRU: Relaxing here.

LYLE: Come here, over here.

PRU: No… Relaxing here.

LYLE: Come stand by me.

PRU: Fine just here. Exhausted.

LYLE: Want you to stand.

PRU: Want to stay sitting.

LYLE: Need you by me here.

PRU: Need to sit. Can and will sit.

LYLE: Lyle says stand by me. By the punch.

PRU: Oh Lyle, let me, for a second...

LYLE: You know what can happen.

PRU: Standing.

Pru stands.

PRU: But I'm staying over here. And then I'm sitting back down.

LYLE: Don't make me be weird. I just want a single moment with you, by my side.

PRU: You're dishevelled. Best to leave it.

LYLE: Best to come here before I cluck and shatter and...

PRU: No more pecker, no more peck...

LYLE: You're not here.

PRU: That's right, I'm over here.

LYLE: Be here now.

PRU: My head hurts Lyle. My feet!

LYLE: For me!! Do it for me!!!!

Pause. She walks to him, they stand by the punch.

LYLE: Can you see right to the bottom of the
punch?

Pru looks in.

PRU: No. Yes. Yes.

LYLE: What do you see?

PRU: Kind of... Nothing.

LYLE: Black.

PRU: Murky.

LYLE: Nothing good.

PRU: This mess we're in.

LYLE: Staaaaaaaaaaaayyyyyyyyyyy!!

*Lyle pushes Pru's head into the punch bowl, holds it down.
Brings it up.*

LYLE: Will you stay?

PRU: Lyle I...

LYLE: Staaaaaayyyyyyyyyy!!

Lyle pushes her head down again.

LYLE: The women in my life. The women in my
life. She was my mother's friend. Tennis friend. They
played on Tuesdays. I was nine. Ten maybe.

Lyle lifts her head up, she's gasping. Puts her back in.

LYLE: She used to come down, after her doubles
match, to the tree, where I'd play, on my own, she'd see me
seeing her, coming.

Lyle lifts her head up. Stares at her.

LYLE: You don't leave Pru. You don't leave.

Lyle pushes her down again.

LYLE: She'd play with it. Kneed it, like pastry,
make it stiffy, then she'd climb on it, mum's friend, fifty
six she was. Diane, from the tuckshop.

Lyle lifts her up. She whales. He puts her back in.

LYLE: She'd move back and forth like a wobbly
bus. Grinding. Squashing my legs. Calling me her little
tiger, her little muscle man. A good childhood. That's what
I need. I might go to seven-eleven, get myself a good
childhood.

Lyle lifts her up.

LYLE: Five six bucks.

*Pru does five or six intermediate karate moves on him,
finishing with a keeyai and bow. Lyle lies on the floor, still.
Pru takes her knickers out of the punch and pulls them over
Lyle's face. Pru goes to the John Farnham portrait, talks to it.*

PRU: Each bird must be observed each and
every day by persons competent to determine if each bird
is "normal" or showing signs of disease or distress. A
healthy bird will be alert, move easily about the pen or
cage, will readily eat, drink, and defecate. A low bird will
stay still and rarely respond. Give up. A high bird will
cluck joyously at every moment of every day.

LYLE: *(joyous)* Cluuuuckkk!

*Danny props up swiftly, holding the lipstick, paints two war
paint like lines under his eyes.*

DANNY: I saw a woman who I thought was my
mother, but maybe it was because she was crossing the
road. I saw a man who I thought was my father, but
maybe that was because I could only see his legs. I saw a
man who I thought was me, but maybe he was just
coughing. I saw a man that I thought was you Lyle, but
maybe he was just staring at me. I saw a woman that
looked like you Pru.

Pause.

DANNY: There was a child out there, in a mid riff,
on a scooter, smoking a cigarette, and laughing at a dog

with three legs, who was trapped under a wheely bin, which sat outside a house, that was yet to let go of Christmas, and I asked her, if anything would happen, and she looked at me and... Is anyone going to take charge... of this room... hold it up?

PRU: There's fireworks on the way.

DANNY: Lyle. Have you anything to proffer?

LYLE: Nope.

DANNY: Nothing? Make me a drink, some punch!

PRU: He's okay, Danny, just let him...

DANNY: Lyle, it's me, and I need drink.

PRU: I'll fix it for you.

DANNY: No! Lyle fix it! Lyle fix it now! Punch!

Pause.

DANNY: Don't' bend it Lyle, stay with me, don't
bend it.

LYLE: We've moved, I'm corporate, growth and
progression, can't fix anymore, people under me, gonna' do
that for me.

PRU: We've made some plans.

DANNY: Filled him full of the cordial again have
you?

PRU: The time has come where both of you have to…

DANNY: We have to do nothing! Like the fucking Buddhists!

PRU: Lyle   has   ambition   and   possibility steaming out his eyes!

DANNY: Lyle   has   lop-sided   and   dysfunctional streaming out his arse!

PRU: I need to see him grow…

DANNY: I need to see him here.

PRU: You think nothing but Danny.

DANNY: I am Danny! There is no one else!

PRU: Let him go Danny! He can make it.

DANNY: Where? Where can he make it to? I'll tell you, two places, first he'll make it into your knickers, which is a dungeon in itself, and then he'll pass go to another place where they fuck your mind. And it'll take me another five years to get him back in this room where he belongs, cos' there is no other rooms for us. There is only this. Why can't people see that, you, the fucking people, cut us off… "They'll be right"… Fucken'… Fucken… Send in the mover's… take the furniture… take the heart…

PRU: I have a job for him at the station in the mail room. He starts Tuesday.

DANNY: There is no Tuesday.

PRU: Tuesday comes after Monday.

DANNY: And Monday never comes.

PRU: Fuck you Danny he's moving.

LYLE: When we were in the pen.

DANNY: Yes.

PRU: Don't let him drag you back Lyle, you're
so close.

LYLE: When we we're in the pen.

DANNY: When we we're in the pen?

LYLE: And we'd been so good, sharing. We only had two chickens left, they had to last, and before we went to sleep we'd share a foot, or an eye, or some neck, or a bit of tail, sometimes we'd eat a whole breast, but that was only after not eating for a long time. Well the night before they found us Danny, we ate the second last leg together, all that was left was one leg, and we'd shared everything. Well, just after you went to sleep... that night, I ate the last leg. And you wouldn't know because they came with the flash lights that night, so you didn't think, but I know, and I remember, I ate it Danny, I kept it all to myself, I chewed the ankle, the foot, the knee, I sucked every last bit of marrow from the leg of that bastard fowl. And I cried as I enjoyed the most glorious single meal of my life.

Pause.

69

DANNY: You see? This is who we are.

LYLE: I'm coming with you, we're going back.

Lyle and Danny come together.

LYLE: We're going in.

DANNY: We're going in.

LYLE: We're in.

Fireworks. Loud chicken screams. Flashes of light. The pen is revealed in flashes. Black.

Two spotlights shine from the black, one on Lyle, one on Danny. Silence. They are ten and twelve, in the chicken pen.

LYLE: She come back?

Pause.

LYLE: Danny, she come back?

Pause.

LYLE: Danny? Danny you hear me? Danny I asked you... where's mum... where's mum...

DANNY: Shhh... I hear something.

LYLE: What is it?

DANNY: Shhh...

Pause.

DANNY: Nothing.

LYLE: Nothing.

Black. Snap lights on Pru, reporting.

PRU: Two school boy's from the Central Tablelands of NSW were discovered in a chicken pen in their backyard today. Police estimate the brother's, aged ten and twelve, had spent somewhere between three and five months in the pen prior to their discovery earlier this morning. The two children were found cowering in the corner, frightened, and unable to speak. They are currently under observation at Our Lady of Mercy Hospital.

Black. Snap lights on Danny and Lyle. Danny is trying to catch the first chicken.

DANNY: It won't die! The damn bird won't die!
Lyle!

LYLE: Die you damn bird!

DANNY: I saw someone kill it on the cartoons. Who
was it?

LYLE: Oh, the hunter guy with the red beard.

DANNY: Yeah, yeah, how'd he kill it?

LYLE: With his rifle.

Danny catches it, hands it to Lyle. Snap light to Pru.

PRU: Maddened by hunger, the boys were driven to desperate acts. Left with no alternative but to murder their chicken pen inmates. We can only imagine what effect brutality of this nature would have on the tender minds of innocent youth.

Black. Spotlights on Lyle and Danny. Spoken and sung at the same time.

DANNY: *(singing)* Georgie Porgie pudding and pie, kissed the girls and made them cry...

LYLE: *(hysterical)* He won't fucking die Danny!!

DANNY: *(singing)* When all the girls came out to play...

LYLE: *(hysterical)* Die you fucker chicken!!

DANNY: *(singing)* Georgie Porgie ran away.

LYLE: Arggghh!!

Lyle stomps on the chickens head. Repetitively. On every stomp he says...

LYLE: Die! Die ! Die! Die!

Black. Light on Pru, reporting.

PRU: Sadly, too many of our youngsters today will experience some form of extreme trauma. Many are subject to abuse: Sexual, physical, psychological. But this particular case has astounded police and experts alike, with its rare brand of horror.

Black. Spotlights on.

DANNY: Ey Lyle, you awake?

LYLE: No.

DANNY: You know Miss Boson, our principal?

LYLE: Yeah.

DANNY: Do you reckon...

LYLE: What?

DANNY: Do you reckon...

LYLE: What? What are you laughing at?

DANNY: Do you reckon she has one of them
vaginas?

Pause.

LYLE: Nup. She'd have something different, only
mum has them.

DANNY: What would she have?

LYLE: She'd have... she'd have...

DANNY: Maybe she'd have...

LYLE: A chicken...

DANNY: ...A chicken.

73

Pause.

DANNY: Missed heaps of homework.

LYLE: Missed the talent quest.

DANNY: And the fun run.

LYLE: Danny?

DANNY: Yeah?

Pause.

LYLE: Does your head jolt forward a little
sometimes?

DANNY: Yeah, and back, does yours?

LYLE: Sometimes.

DANNY: It's probably because we always…

LYLE: It's probably cos' we…

DANNY: Miss Boson's got a chicken.

Pause.

DANNY: Don't cry Lyle.

LYLE: I want some milk, and some biscuits, and
some television.

DANNY: She'll be back soon, she's probably just gone up to the pub for bingo. She does that some Tuesdays.

LYLE: But it's more than Tuesday.

DANNY: She probably just forgot, she'll get us, she feeds em' all the time, she'll get us.

LYLE: I dunno'. I reckon she's fucked off.

DANNY: No! Mum wouldn't fuck off, she's got too much going on, the phone's always ringin' guys always ringin' her, guys always comin' round, in suits, serious guys.

LYLE: Mum's left us.

DANNY: She's just gone to bingo and had too much Moselle.

LYLE: I'm hungry!

DANNY: So eat the wire, she'll be here.

LYLE: Soooo hungry…

DANNY: You're not hungry, you just think you are, think of all the food you've ever eaten, you can't be hungry.

LYLE: I want some cordial! Muuuuuummmm!!

Pause.

DANNY: *(singing)* Georgie Porgie, pudding and pie...

LYLE: Someone!!!!!

Black. Pru reporting.

PRU: Disturbing development today in the story of the "Twin Beaks". Psychologists have reported that the two boys may have become irreversably chemically aligned. A terrifying prospect. These boys should either be separated immediately, or never separated again. It's as simple as that.

Black. Spotlights.

DANNY: Lyle.

LYLE: Yes Danny.

DANNY: Lyle.

LYLE: Yes Danny.

DANNY: How many fingers?

LYLE: Three.

DANNY: Lyle.

LYLE: Yes Danny.

DANNY: Lyle.

LYLE: Chicken or the egg.

DANNY: Lyle.

LYLE: Yes Danny.

DANNY: Chicken or the egg.

LYLE: Chicken.

DANNY: Lyle

LYLE: Yes Danny.

DANNY: Lyle.

LYLE: Yes Danny.

DANNY: Cluck.

LYLE: Cluck.

DANNY: Lyle.

LYLE: Yes Danny.

DANNY: Who's a silly fucker?

Pause.

DANNY: Lyle?

LYLE: Yes Danny?

DANNY: Who's a silly fucker?

LYLE: I am.

DANNY: Can't hear you.

LYLE: Danny?

DANNY: Yes Lyle.

Pause.

LYLE: We could dig our way out of here you
know. I reckon we could.

Pause.

DANNY: Lyle!?

LYLE: Yes Danny?

DANNY: Who's a silly fucker!?

LYLE: I am!

DANNY: Who's a silly fucker!?

LYLE: I am!

DANNY: Can't hear you?!

LYLE: I'm a silly fucker!

Black. Pru.

PRU: Now safely in protective care, our boys
will begin the long and arduous journey back to humanity.
Fed everything but chicken, and exposed to all television
but cartoons the news and shows about the zoo. A

dedicated team of Nutritional Psychologists have devised a unique treatment plan. Televisions a big no no, and chicken, is definitely off the menu.

Black. Harsh spotlights.

DANNY: You shat yourself in the clubhouse, before the football game. Against Bosco. I saw the brown in the white.

LYLE: I didn't.

DANNY: You got a dick like a cornetto...

LYLE: I don't...

DANNY: You're an albino.

LYLE: I'm not.

DANNY: Your un-co. Nobody picks you. Always last.

LYLE: I'm good at things.

DANNY: You say stupid things, you're dumb like shit.

LYLE: I'm good.

DANNY: And you're a pussy in a fight, Dave Stewart fucked you up.

LYLE: Dave Stewart's Tongan.

DANNY: And you're a poofter, you're a gay poofter.

LYLE: I'm not, I'm tough like bricks.

DANNY: You're a lesbian gay un-co ugly retard shit yourself albino fuckhead!

LYLE: I'm not, I'm good. I'm good.

DANNY: You're a shit stick, dick rash, fuck nose, lesbian, bum licker.

LYLE: So why do you hang around me all the time?

DANNY: Cos I'm stuck in a fucking chicken pen with you!

Black. Pru.

PRU: Inevitably, as months went by, the physicality of the brother's moved more into that of the chicken, than that of the young man, and as starvation became more and more vicious, killing for survival became a necessity. And it is common knowledge, that chickens do not die easy.

Black. Spotlights. Crying.

DANNY: Goodnight Stock.

LYLE: Goodnight Stock.

DANNY: You die hard Stock.

LYLE: You tough chook Stock.

DANNY: But goodnight.

LYLE: Goodnight.

DANNY: We eat you with love Stock.

LYLE: We eat your eyeballs first.

DANNY: Out of love.

Blue liquid dribbles down their cheeks. They smile.

DANNY: Why did the chicken cross the road?

Pause.

LYLE: I dunno.

Pause.

LYLE: Why?

Pause.

DANNY: Cos' he could.

Silence.

LYLE: Imagine crossing the road.

DANNY: Wow.

Black. Pru.

PRU: And finally, on a happy note, what about the age of reason? Since the release of the chicken boys last week, great Australian artists such as Ken Done and John Farnham have rallied together organizing concerts and exhibitions to raise funds for their continuing care. Also lending a hand is Jenny Kee who today launched "Jolly Jumpers for Life". Jenny hopes to get school children across the country to join their jumpers and cardigans together, making a giant colourful mural which will be visible from outer space. Yay, team Australia!

Black. Spotlights. Slow tremor.

DANNY: Cluck.

LYLE: Cluck, cluck.

DANNY: Cluck, cluck, cluck.

LYLE: Cluck, cluck, cluck, cluck.

DANNY: Cluck.

LYLE: Cluck, cluck.

DANNY: Cluck, cluck.

LYLE: Cluck.

DANNY: Cluck?

Pause.

LYLE: Cluck.

Pause. Tremor builds.

LYLE: Cluck, cluck cluck cluck cluck.

Pause.

DANNY: Cluck. Cluck! Cluck!

Pause. Tremor close to climax.

DANNY: Cluck! Cluck! Cluck!!!!

LYLE: Cluuuuuuccckkk!!!!!

Silence. Flash lights get stronger, tremor builds, the boy's cluck louder in fear. Suddenly there's garish light and the boy's are blinded. They scuttle like frightened chickens erratic all over the stage. Lights flash and find them. They are maddened, and intensely bewildered. Tremor builds. Fireworks. Not knowing what to do or where to go, the boys begin to peck each other savagely. Danny eventually wins. Pecking Lyle to the ground. Black.

Light. Television studio. Current affair theme. Pru prepares to go back on air. 5 – 4 – 3 - 2

PRU: So much for the Aussie Battler. Now, a much anticipated story. Making their first television appearance since the horrible chicken pen asylum of seven years ago, are brothers Danny and Lyle, please, welcome to The Hard Line, Danny and Lyle.

AUDIENCE APPLAUSE. Enter Danny and Lyle, 16 and 18. They sit.

PRU: How are you this evening gentleman?

DANNY: Yeah, good.

LYLE: Umm, yeah... fine.

PRU: You look great. It's amazing, since word got out that you would be appearing on The Hard Line, letters have flooded the station, and the phones have been red hot with public interest, intrigue, and sympathy. Are you aware of the place you have in the heart of Australians?

DANNY: We've had some nice letters from old ladies.

PRU: Do you like your new found fame?

DANNY: Oh it's not... it's not... fame.

PRU: What do Danny and Lyle do in their down time?

DANNY: Down... time? What's down... time?

LYLE: We're not down.

PRU: Let me rephrase that.

LYLE: We're not down. We're up.

PRU: Spare time. Sports? Music? Lyle?

Pause.

LYLE: I don't like music. Danny said, that, Danny you said. Danny said he'd be interested... in learning how to play the oboe.

DANNY: Yeah, it'd be alright.

Pause.

PRU: Would you say, in a word, that you were happy people?

Pause.

DANNY: Um, I can only speak for myself, cos' I'm not Lyle. But, um... yeah.

Pause.

PRU: Right, and you Lyle, are you?

LYLE: Um, well, pretty weird, I don't know. I don't really know what's real.

PRU: I speak for the whole of Australia when I say this, we are so grateful that you've come on the show to share your story. What was it that made your mind up to come on the show?

Pause.

PRU: Danny?

LYLE: The money and the flat you got us?

DANNY: You... You. We said we'd do it if it was you.

PRU: And I'm appropriately flattered. Now that you are here, and in the lounge rooms of Australia, is there anything you'd like to say?

DANNY: I can only say that... and I speak for myself only cos' Lyle is who he is. But... I can't really function in the normal world, on the street, everyone knows who you are, and they tend to be scared you're going to peck them or something.

Canned laughter.

LYLE: We didn't choose it. It just happened.

DANNY: My grandfather was in Vietnam and he got a similar reaction when he came home.

PRU: Have you had any contact with your mother since the event?

DANNY: Nup.

PRU: Do you feel at all, angry with her?

Pause.

PRU: Lyle?

LYLE: Yeah. I hate her. Hate.

PRU: What would you say to her if you could, if she was watching?

86

Pause.

PRU: Okay. Ok.

Pause.

PRU: Do you feel in any way…

LYLE: What are you getting at bitch?!

PRU: Nothing, I'm just asking the appropriate questions.

LYLE: You said in the green room, before the interview, you'd ask us a few questions about a few things and then we could get a limousine back to our fucken flat. We don't want to talk mum and chicken. We want money, limo, free shit, and some fucking respect.

DANNY: Lyle, simmer down mate we're on television.

LYLE: We're on television every time we leave the fucking house! This is no different.

PRU: Let's start again, I'm sorry Lyle.

Pause.

PRU: How do you feel about other children who've had similar experiences in confined spaces?

LYLE: Everyone's been in a confined space, cos' everyone's been in the womb. Ask a decent question.

Lyle stands up.

DANNY: Lyle sit down... Lyle! Sit!

LYLE: Not sitting. My name is Lyle.

DANNY: Lyle, sit down!

LYLE: I know what you all think of me, and I know why you do, cos' it's easier that way, it's easier to see me as the freak, than have an honest look into my eyes and see what you've done to me. What you do to all of us. You kill us as you turn the page. Win a hamper, win a car, goodbye, you're the weakest chicken, win a soul, who's got new tits? Who's a size fourteen, who threw a TV out the window, I got brochures in my head, I got fourteen channels digitizing disintegration in prime time Lyle's mind, you kill me, you make me plastic puppet and you paint me pastel poison, you kill me, as you suck the nipple change the channel, and me and my brother, we didn't even chose this, we fucken' didn't! We don't want this! But you kill us anyway! You kill us as you make us more than you. But I am more than you. I'm a fucking chicken, and I stand un-pecked at the top of the pecking order, and not one of you impassive aliens can knock me down, cos' doin' time in that pen built a perspex shield between me and your filthy sentiments, I'm untouchable now, you can't touch me at all, you can't pause me rewind me, nothin! So crack another beer and ignore your wife for another year, I know what it's like to be alive, cos I'm a fucking chicken! I've got parts of myself that I'd like to vote off the island! I'm as ugly as the next guy! Let's cover it up! Cover it all up! With a gun to my head and a muffin in my mouth! Let's cover it all up! Turn your problems on! Turn your problems off! Lucky man in a lucky country! Para Olympic

Mardi Gras and Cold Wars and hot baths! Cover it all up! You're not okay! You should not be able to sleep! You should not be able to sleep! Why am I what you want? To laugh at, to have, comparison, am I war to you, am I easy, am I comfort, to know, you'll know never know what I know!? Cover me up! Cover the fuck! Freak! What's a freak!? What's a freak!? Leave me alone to cluck... be alone... Cluck... Leave me alone to be alone... I just want to... cluck... live. Please!? I... I... Please!? Cluck... Cluck! Cluck!

Lyle is cut off by the network. Black.

Lights up. Pru is massaging punch into Danny's bare shoulders. He has the loop earring on.

DANNY: This room knows what's going on. I feel it, staring at me, disapproving. So bare and clunky.

PRU: 11:51.

DANNY: There's some change coming, the room knows, I know.

PRU: Change.

Pause. She pours punch on his head, like a sacrament.

DANNY: Sportsgirl... Out the window... Her little ritual... She bailed out of BMW... Straddled the bubbler... Clean the dungeon... And back again... On it... Skirt hitched hand out... To service... She caught me... And down I go... Your fish net eyes in her fish net skull... And she was you... Without having to be me...

89

Silence. Pru pours more punch on his head.

PRU: We really gotta' take some time, get away, breathe each other in again. Cos' it's moving so fast, time, and we're getting past where we make sense. We have to join again, remember when we used to lie there, and stare each other down, peer into each other, fearless and open... and we saw everything, the black, the gold, and we loved it all. We really gotta' take some time.

DANNY: You oppress me.

PRU: If we take one more step away from each other, we won't be able to reach.

DANNY: Can't reach.

PRU: Can't touch.

DANNY: Can't feel...

PRU: Anything.

DANNY: Nothing you say...

PRU: Means anything.

DANNY: It's all...

PRU: Television.

Pause.

DANNY: It's fucking useless being with someone that isn't you.

Pause. She pours more punch over his head. A shower blares into action from off.

DANNY: Fucking useless.

Pause.

PRU: New year soon. Happy new one.

Pause.

PRU: I have money.

DANNY: Don't want it.

PRU: Just for a little while, get you started...

DANNY: You oppress me.

PRU: I'm helping you...

DANNY: You're helping me...

PRU: Be more!

DANNY: For what? For whom? For how?

PRU: For beautiful us?!

DANNY: For beautiful us.

PRU: Come on and try...

DANNY: Try my best...

PRU: The best you can...

DANNY: You oppress me.

Pause. Shower singing Lyle. She pours more.

PRU: I won't die that easy.

DANNY: Hard to kill.

PRU: I know you love me...

DANNY: I know you do.

PRU: You make mistakes...

DANNY: Thrive on them.

PRU: Come with me...

DANNY: To wonderland.

PRU: Make a baby.

DANNY: Chicken or egg?

PRU: You can trust me.

DANNY: You oppress me.

Pause. Shower stops. She pours more.

PRU: I can't hang on to nothing Danny.

Pause.

PRU: You've almost broke me.

Pause. An electric shaver hums from off.

PRU: I'm technically knocked out.

Pause.

The buzzing stops. Silence. A hair drier blows from off. She pours on his head.

PRU: Come with me Danny, we'll make strong...

DANNY: It happened to me Pru, I didn't witness it.

PRU: Grow...

DANNY: It's in me Pru, it's mine.

PRU: I live in this fucking machine...

DANNY: See that it's mine Pru.

PRU: A machine that began with beauty, began with you, made me truth teller, and now the mobiles chirp, and the money in the box is me...

DANNY: This is mine. This is what I have.

PRU: I don't get younger...

DANNY: I'll kill anything close to me Pru.

PRU: Let me care for it.

DANNY: Outside. The suicidal struggle of cigarette's and cold vaginas. There's a duty, to keep it close, keep it family...

PRU: Our family...

Pause. Electric tooth brush starts from off. She pours. Silence.

DANNY: There's not much I've really ever felt. But I feel something now.

She entwines herself on him, on the chair. He rocks her like a baby in a blanket.

PRU: Come with me Danny.

DANNY: When nothing happens at all, for a long time, a whole lot of things happen. You know, there's something I owe you, and you owe me, a duty, a fucking duty, to look after me, to scrape me off the gutter and put me in a hospital, to lift me from the ground and out of the bar, to help me from the black and into the light, and there's a duty, a fucking duty, that we owe to each other, to do that. Walk the baby, hold the dog, walk the baby, hold the dog... you don't leave, you don't live a life of, I remember a father, then a stranger, with a reading voice for a reading night he'd read, to us, and then be gone, and a mother, moves in, and the stranger gone, and the father gone, and there's a duty, it was like central fucking station, my house, and we have to look after each other, it's plain fucking humanity, scrape each other off the gutter, save each other's lives, fuck it, anything! We can do, to help. Where did the father go?! Where did the stranger's go?! Who was the stranger, he came, he read, he fucking left, and there's a duty, to stay, to be there, and men are Gods, and men are Gods, I remember you... you made us feel you, know you, and you no more, just buzz around my head every now and mum, who and where and why and there's a duty, to try, to... But there's a lot of pressure, there's nowhere, no room, no allowance, the government, or... the yeah, the government, I don't know, my mother never home, always men, in suits, coming over turning off the television, with smiles lollies and fast shadows she'd disappear into suits, from a nightgown, made of hair curlers, and there's a duty, from all humans, not to lock each other away, but I understand, the pressure, on all single mother's, not to crack and kill a chair, or iron their arm off, or rattle the crying baby til' it's head falls off, and silence, there's a duty, from one, person, to the next, to fucking, do something, to keep the light in, and the chooks away. There's a duty, a fucking duty. From you to me. There's a duty...

PRU: I do... Danny... I can see... you are...

DANNY: There's a duty, there's a fucking duty...

Silence, they cry and kiss. Enter Lyle, in a suit, looking superb.

LYLE: Well I'm out of here.

Pause.

LYLE: No need to respond. I'm confident enough in my own intentions.

Pause. Lyle stands by the door. He holds a briefcase.

LYLE: I'll call you when I get somewhere...

Pause.

LYLE: Never was good at goodbyes.

Pause.

LYLE: Bye bye jailer.

Pause.

LYLE: Now.

PRU: The irons hot.

LYLE: Fast.

PRU: Respect.

LYLE: Invincible.

PRU: Architecture.

DANNY: Lyle.

LYLE: Exit.

PRU: Disappear.

LYLE: Precisely.

PRU: Blossom.

DANNY: Lyle.

LYLE: Danny.

PRU: Go.

LYLE: Going.

PRU: Try.

LYLE: Trying.

PRU: The best you can.

LYLE: Go team Lyle. Go on and try.

Pause. Lyle steps into the doorway.

DANNY: Remember what I taught you.

LYLE: Inside the pen. Outside the pen. It's all the same.

Pause.

LYLE: I was thinking more of the suave learner, the big giver, the lover of all eyes.

DANNY: All eyes are dead.

LYLE: I gotta' try.

PRU: The best you can.

LYLE: To your health!

DANNY: Hold onto yourself.

Lyle takes a breath.

LYLE: Free to go.

PRU: Free as a bird.

DANNY: White bird.

Pause.

LYLE: Trust.

Pause.

LYLE: Trust.

Pause.

PRU: Proud of Lyle.

LYLE: Sure thing.

PRU: Watch him go.

LYLE: Lyle the goer.

DANNY: Lyle.

PRU: Lyle:

LYLE: Lyle the leaver.

Pause.

PRU: Leave.

LYLE: Leaving.

Pause. Lyle turns.

DANNY: Who's a silly fucker?

Lyle stops. Silence.

LYLE: I figure I'll just saunter out there, and within a short space of time a few corporate types will have picked me up. On the sheer grace of my appearance.

Silence.

DANNY: Lyle.

LYLE: Yes Danny.

DANNY: Lyle.

LYLE: Yes Danny.

DANNY: Who's a silly…

LYLE: Not me Danny.

DANNY: Lyle.

LYLE: Yes Danny.

DANNY: Lyle!

LYLE: Yes Danny.

DANNY: Who's a silly fucker?!

PRU: This is such a surprise.

DANNY: Lyle.

LYLE: Danny.

DANNY: Lyle.

LYLE: Danny?

DANNY: Who's a silly fucker?

LYLE: Not me Danny.

PRU: I never expected this.

DANNY: Lyle.

LYLE: Yes Danny.

DANNY: Who's a silly fucker?

LYLE: Not me Danny.

PRU: I'd like to thank the network.

DANNY: Lyle!

PRU: And the academy.

DANNY: Lyle.

LYLE: Yes Danny?

DANNY: Who's a silly fucker?

LYLE: Not Lyle.

PRU: I ask you to join me now.

DANNY: Who's a silly fucker?

LYLE: No.

DANNY: Who's a silly fucker?

LYLE: Please no.

DANNY: Who's a silly fucker!?

LYLE: Nooo!!

PRU: In a moments silence.

DANY: Who's a silly fucker?

LYLE: Not me. Not me.

DANNY: Who's a silly fucker?

PRU: To celebrate the lives...

DANNY: Who's a silly fucker?

PRU: Of these two men...

DANNY: Lyle!

PRU: Glorious men.

DANNY: Who's a silly fucker?

LYLE: Not me Danny.

DANNY:	Who's a silly fucker?
LYLE:	No Danny.
DANNY:	Who's a silly fucker?
LYLE:	Not me!!
DANNY:	Who's a...
LYLE:	No!
DANNY:	Who's a s...
LYLE:	No!
DANNY:	Who's a silly fucker?!
LYLE:	I am.
DANNY:	Can't hear you?!
LYLE:	I am.
DANNY:	Who's a silly fucker?
LYLE:	I am Danny.
DANNY:	Who's a silly fucker?
LYLE:	I am Danny. I'm a silly fucker.
PRU:	Thank you Australia.
DANNY:	Who's a silly fucker?

LYLE:	I am Danny. I'm a silly fucker.
PRU:	For allowing me the chance…
DANNY:	Lyle.
LYLE:	I am.
PRU:	To achieve the dream.
DANNY:	Can't hear you?
LYLE:	My name is Lyle, and I am a silly fucker.

Pause.

DANNY:	Can you see to the bottom?
PRU:	Grief is brief.
LYLE:	Oh I can see.
DANNY:	They cut us off.
LYLE:	Switched us off.
DANNY:	No alternative.
LYLE:	Men are gods
LYLE:	Goodbye my brother. See you in the cluck.
DANNY:	Goodbye my brother. See you in the cluck.

LYLE/DANNY: Cluck.

Black. Light on punch. Danny and Lyle are behind it.

LYLE: Ten.

DANNY: Nine.

LYLE: Eight.

DANNY: Seven.

LYLE: Six.

DANNY: Five. Cluck.

LYLE: Four.

DANNY: Three.

LYLE: Two. Cluck.

DANNY: One!!

LYLE/DANNY: Happy new!!

Danny and Lyle enter their heads into the punch bowl.
Silence. Drowning.
Dead.
Black.
Pru switches a light on.
Pru goes to the John Farnham signed portrait. She takes it off the wall and reveals a digital video camera. Looks at the boys.
Stillness.
Black.
End.